PAUL McCARTNEY
KISSES ON THE BOTTOM

ISBN 978-1-4584-4063-1

HAL•LEONARD®
CORPORATION

7777 W. BLUEMOUND RD. P.O. BOX 13819 MILWAUKEE, WI 53213

Visit Hal Leonard Online at
www.halleonard.com

I'M GONNA SIT RIGHT DOWN AND WRITE MYSELF A LETTER

Lyric by JOE YOUNG
Music by FRED E. AHLERT

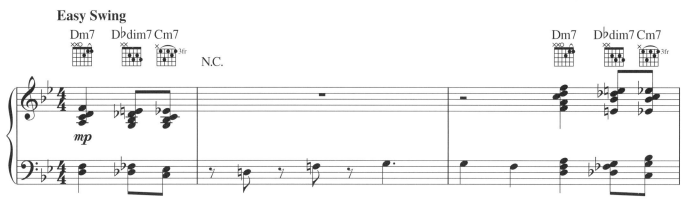

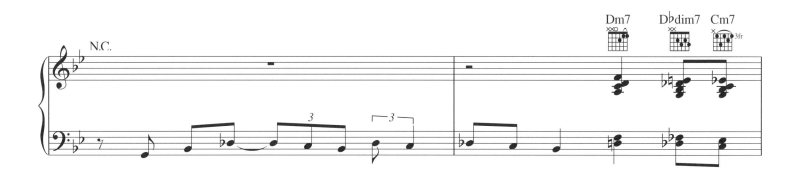

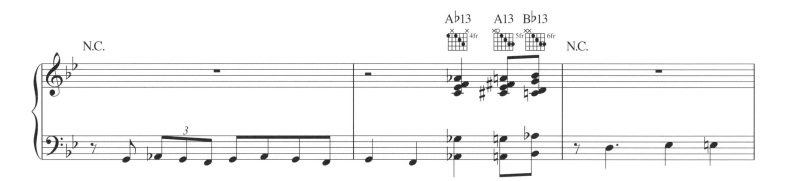

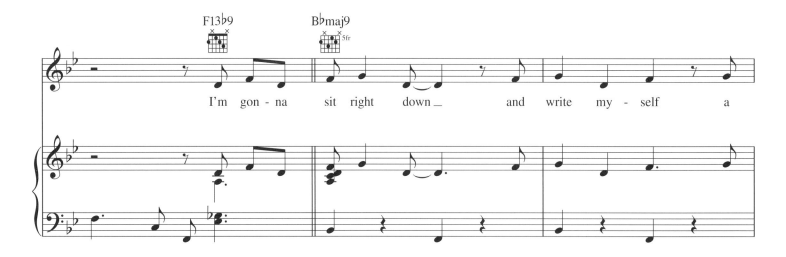

I'm gon-na sit right down ___ and write my-self a

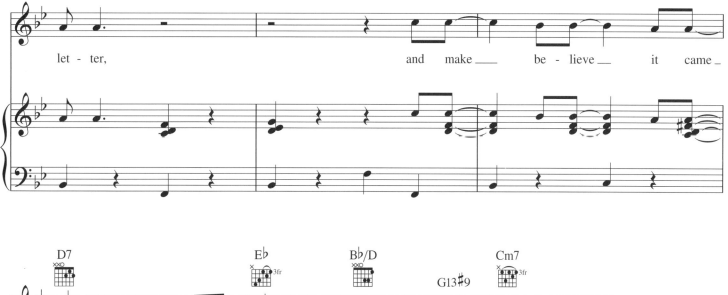

let - ter, and make ___ be - lieve ___ it came ___

___ from you. ___ I'm gon - na

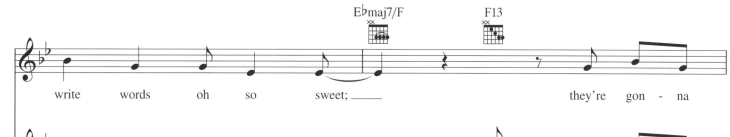

write words oh so sweet; ___ they're gon - na

knock me off my feet. ___ A lot of kiss - es on the bot -

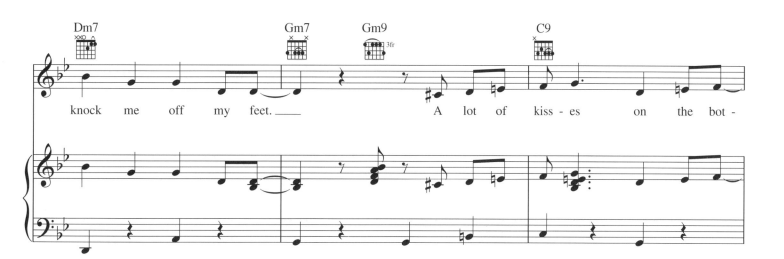

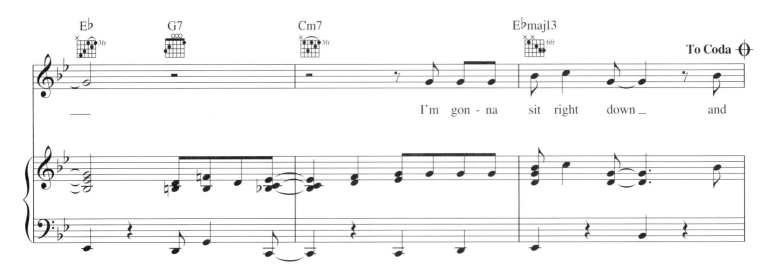

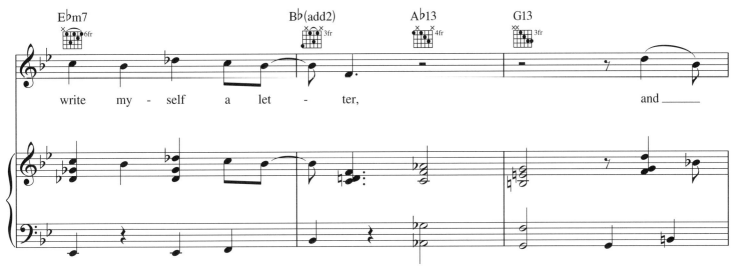

write my - self a let - ter, and ____

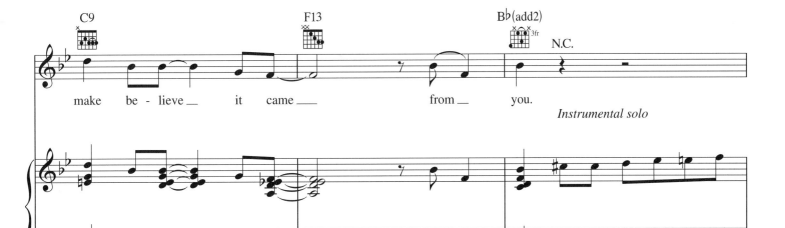

make be - lieve ___ it came ___ from ___ you.

Instrumental solo

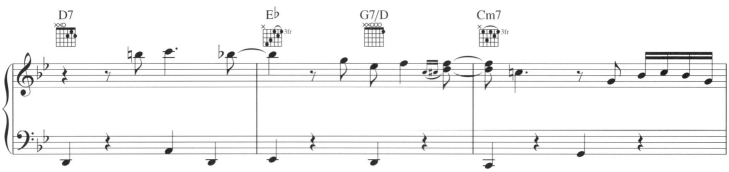

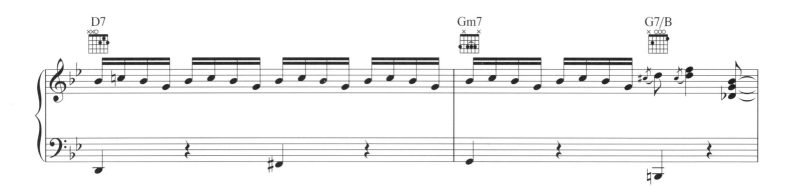

D.S. al Coda

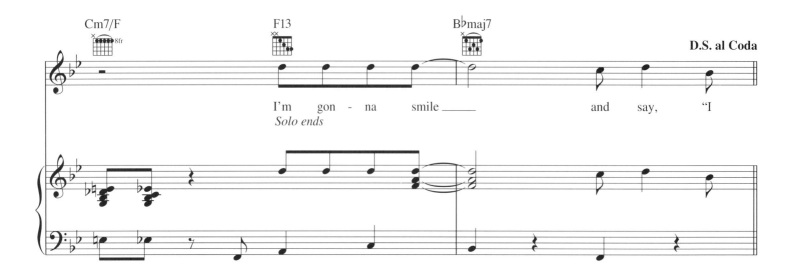

I'm gon - na smile _____ and say, "I

Solo ends

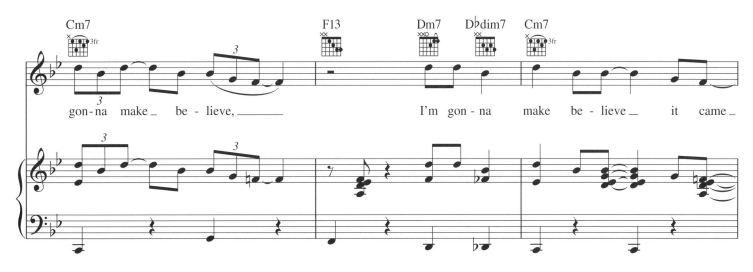

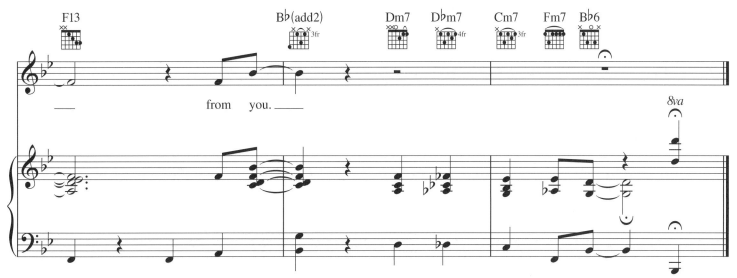

CODA

write my - self a let - ter,

and _____ make be - lieve, _ oh, ___ I'm

gon - na make _ be - lieve, _____ I'm gon - na make be - lieve _ it came _

_ from you. _

HOME
(When Shadows Fall)

Words and Music by GEOFF CLARKSON,
HARRY CLARKSON and PETER VAN STEEDEN

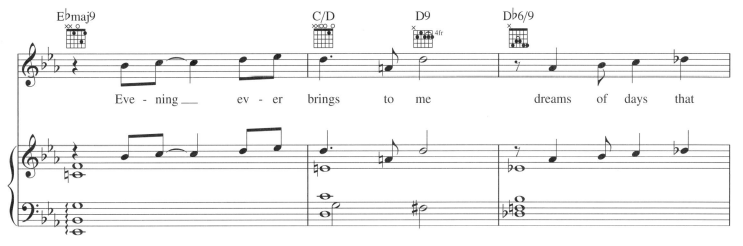

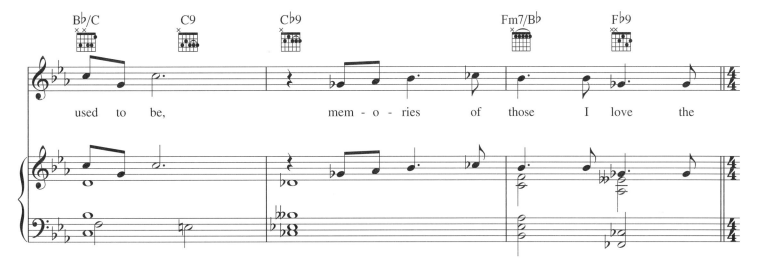

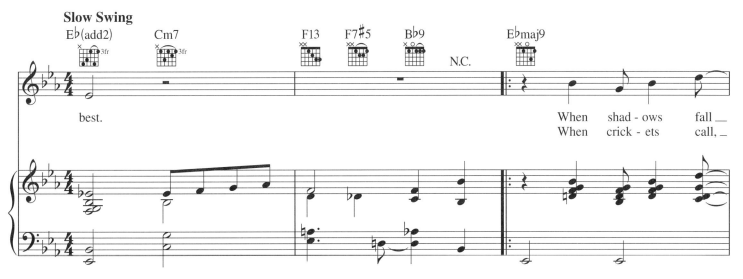

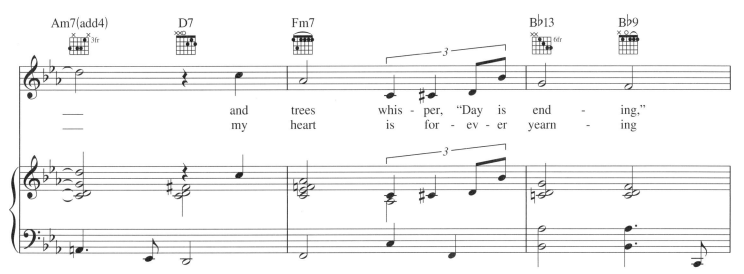

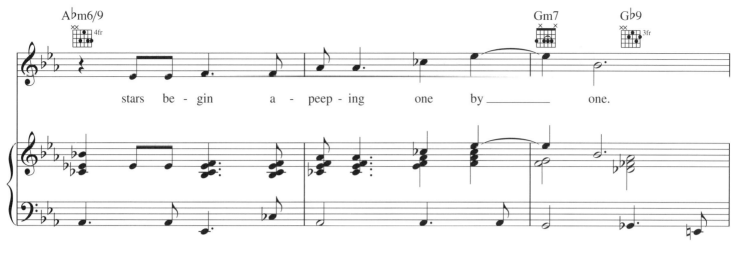

stars be-gin a-peep-ing one by _____ one.

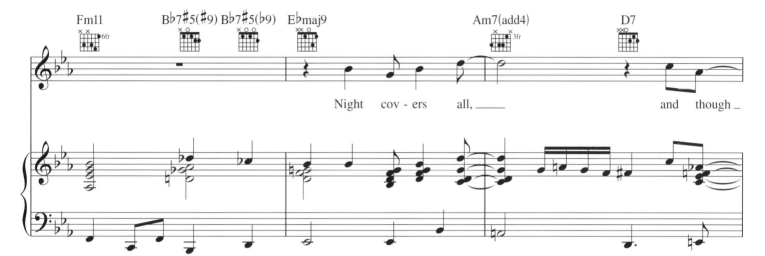

Night cov-ers all, _____ and though _

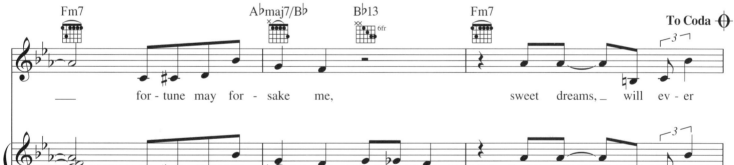

_____ for-tune may for-sake me, sweet dreams, _ will ev-er

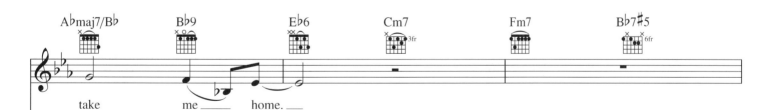

take me _____ home. _____

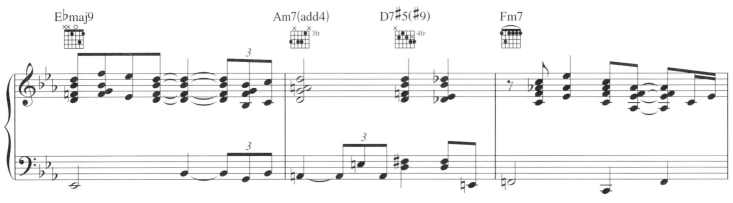

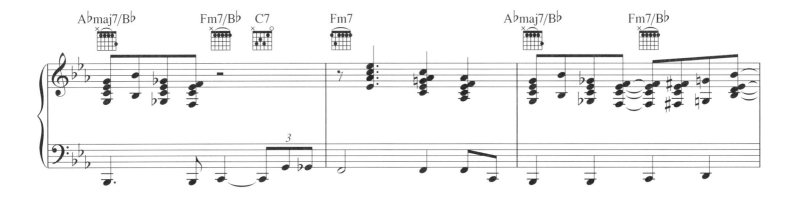

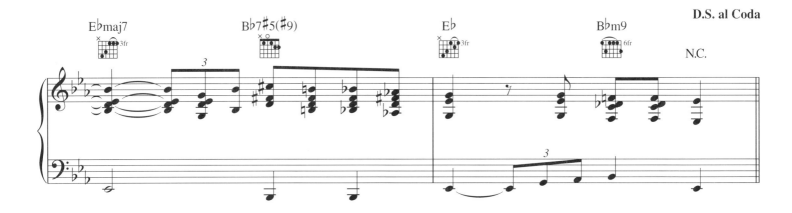

D.S. al Coda

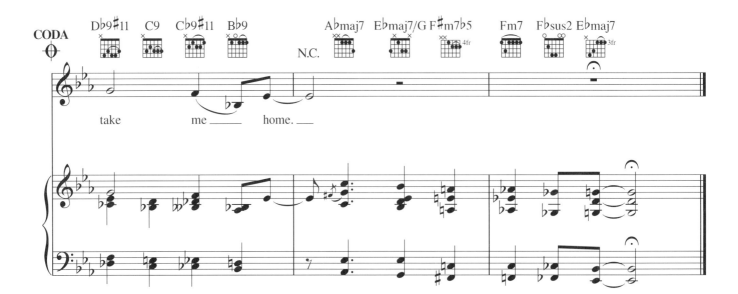

take me _____ home. _____

IT'S ONLY A PAPER MOON

Lyric by BILLY ROSE and E.Y. "YIP" HARBURG
Music by HAROLD ARLEN

Ah yes, it's on-ly a can-vas sky ___ hang-ing o-ver a

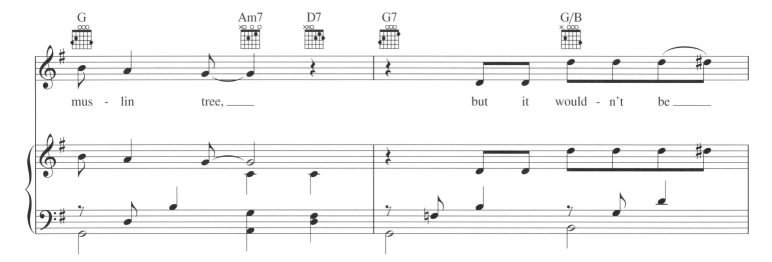

mus-lin tree, ___ but it would-n't be ___

make-be-lieve ___ if you be-lieved in me. ___
Solo ends With-out ___

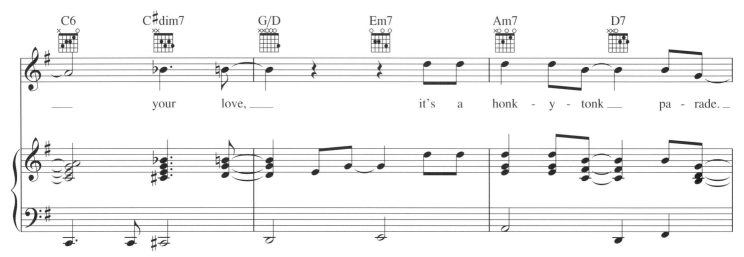

___ your love, ___ it's a honk-y-tonk ___ pa-rade. ___

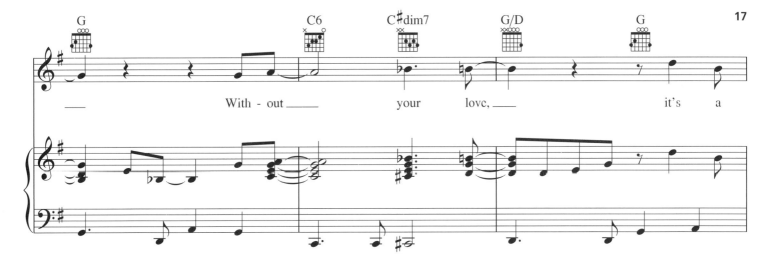

With - out ____ your love, ____ it's a

mel - o - dy played ____ in a pen ny ar - cade. ____

It's a Bar - num and Bai - ley world, ___ just as pho - ny a - bout as pho - ny as

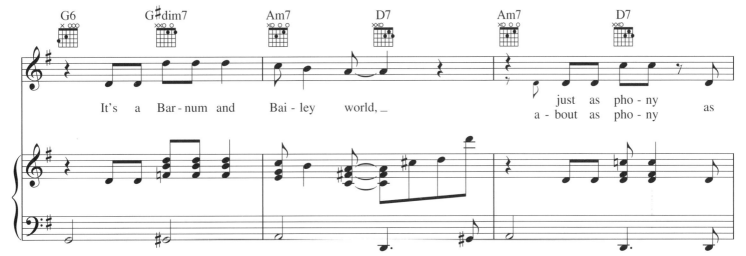

it can be, _____ but it would - n't be _____

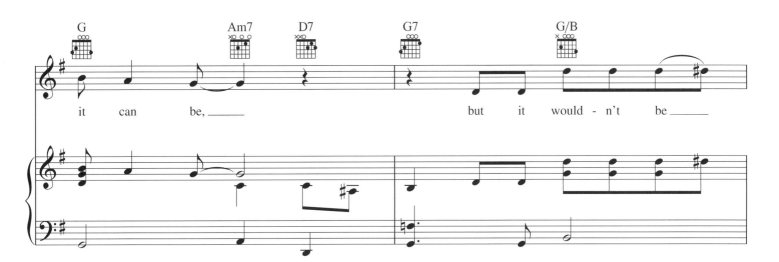

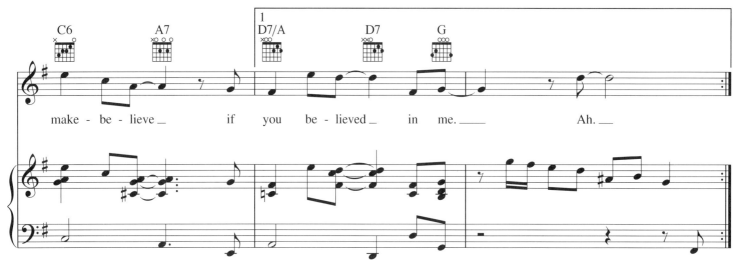

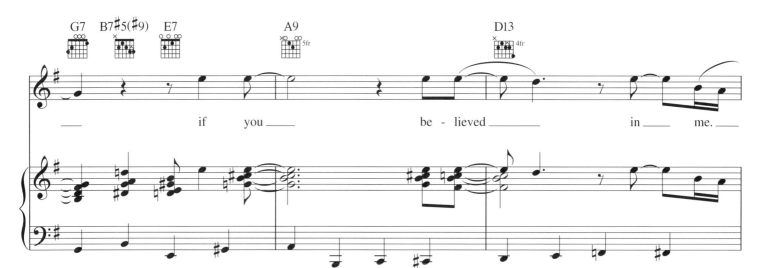

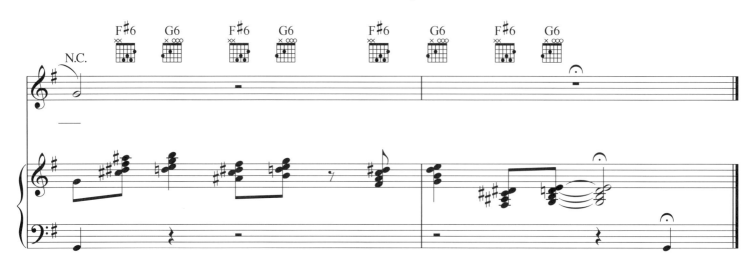

MORE I CANNOT WISH YOU

from GUYS AND DOLLS

By FRANK LOESSER

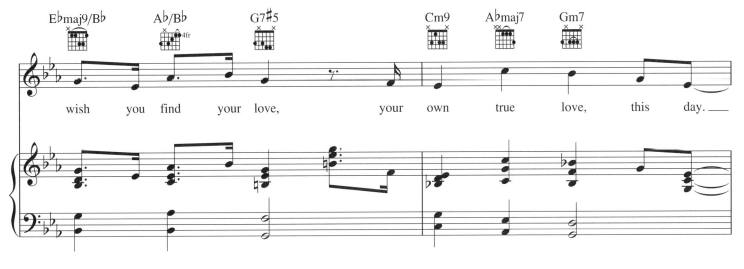

wish you find your love, your own true love, this day. ___

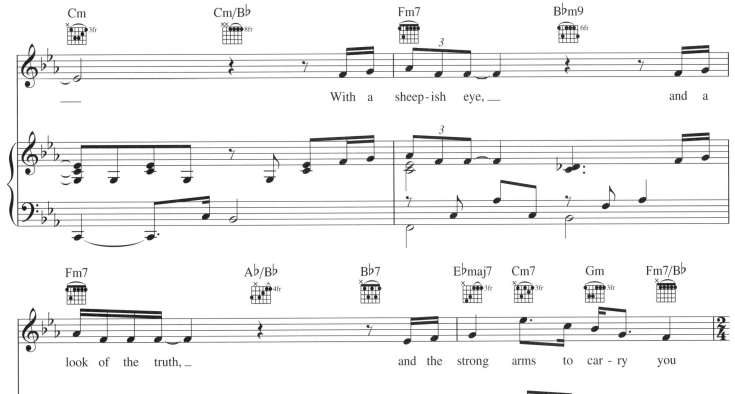

___ With a sheep-ish eye, ___ and a

look of the truth, ___ and the strong arms to car-ry you

Slowly and freely

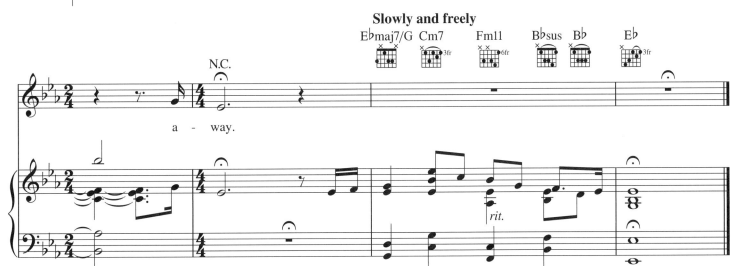

a - way.

THE GLORY OF LOVE

Words and Music by
BILLY HILL

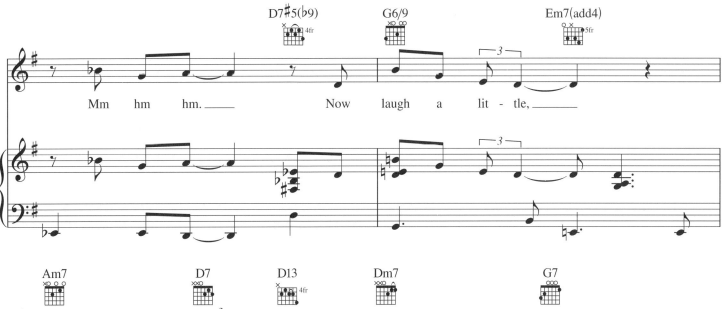

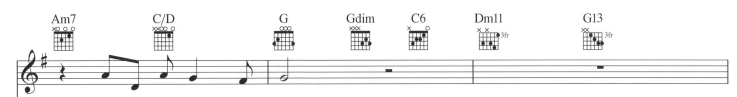

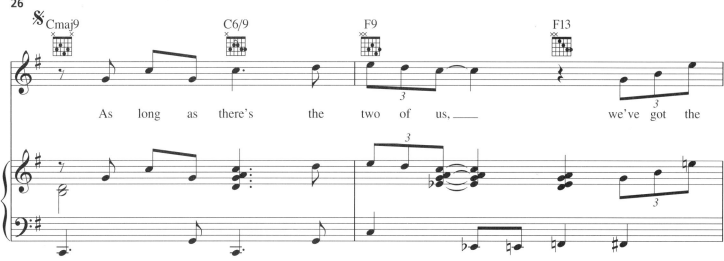

As long as there's the two of us, _____ we've got the

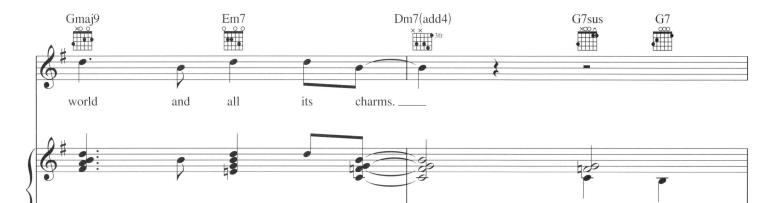

world and all its charms. _____

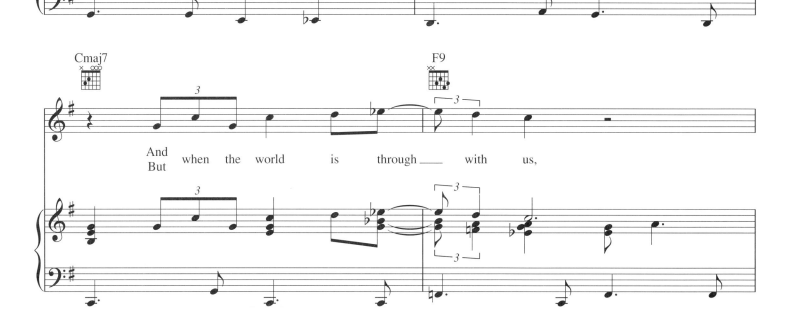

And
But when the world is through _____ with us,

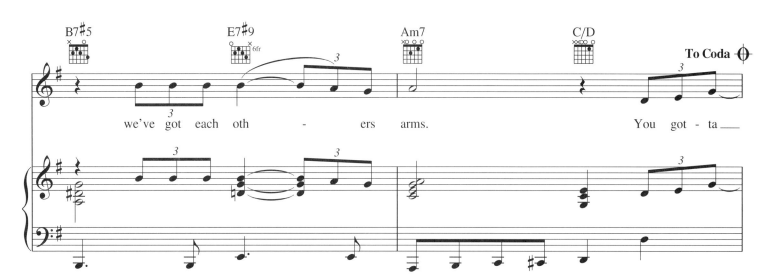

we've got each oth - ers arms. You got - ta _____

To Coda ⊕

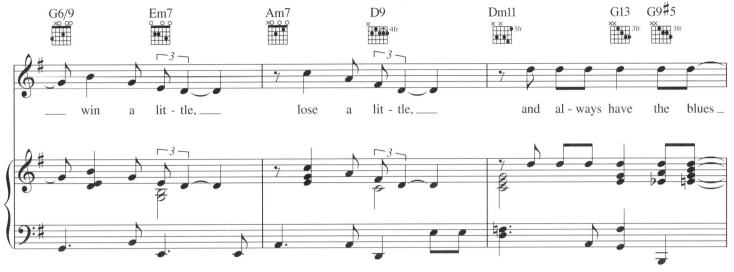

win a lit - tle, __ lose a lit - tle, __ and al - ways have the blues __

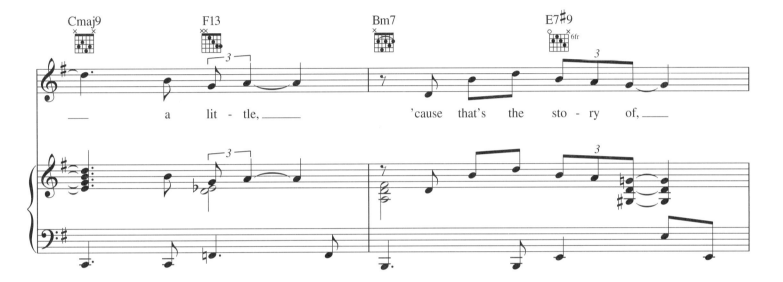

__ a lit - tle, _____ 'cause that's the sto - ry of, ___

yeah that's the glo - ry of love.

Instrumental solo

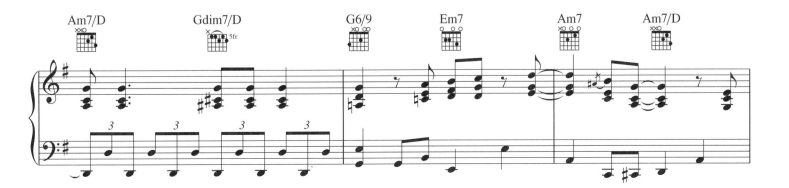

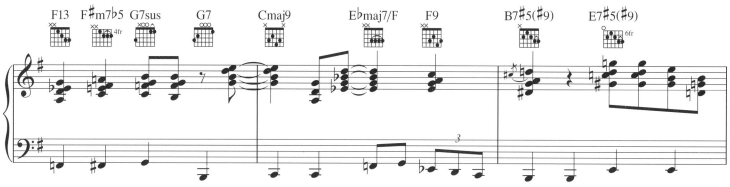

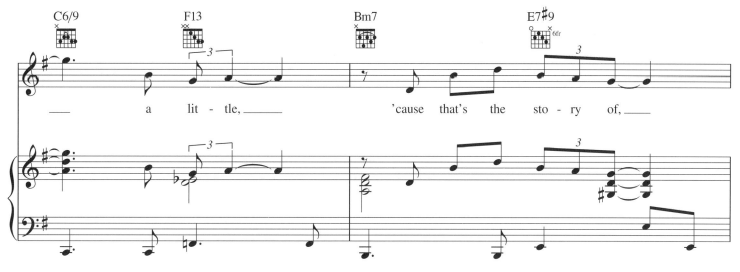

a lit - tle, ___ 'cause that's the sto - ry of, ___

yeah that's the glo - ry of love.

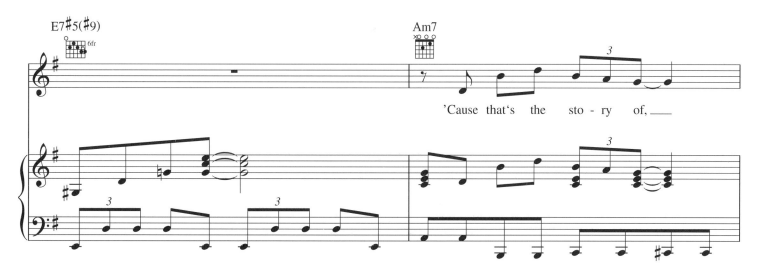

'Cause that's the sto - ry of, ___

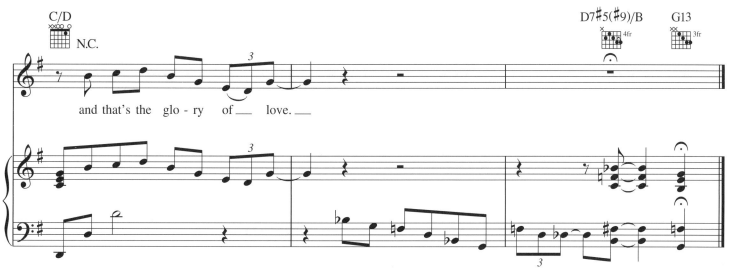

and that's the glo - ry of ___ love. ___

WE THREE
(My Echo, My Shadow and Me)

Lyric and Music by DICK ROBERTSON,
NELSON COGANE and SAMMY MYSELS

Moderately slow Swing

With pedal

We three, _____ we're _ all a-lone, liv-ing _____ in a _____ mem-o-ry; _____ my ech-o, my shad-ow and me. _____

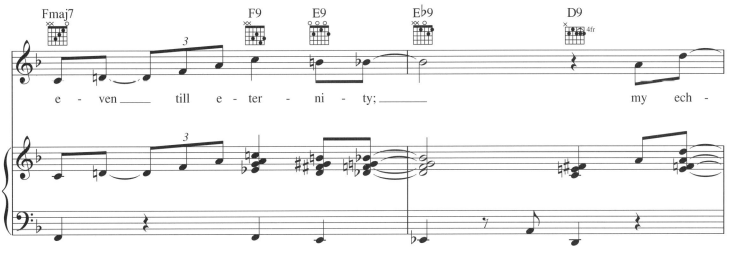

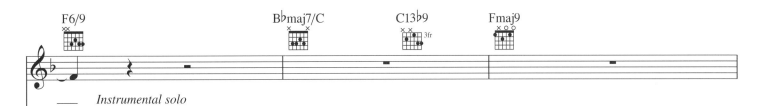

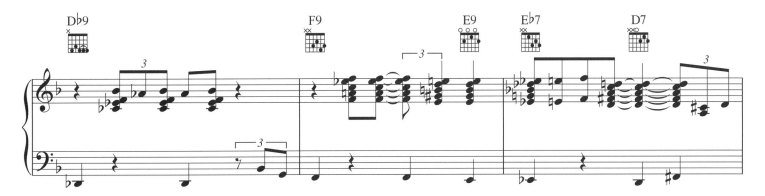

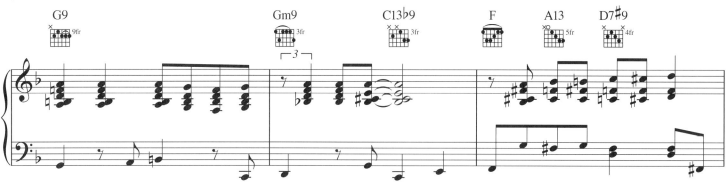

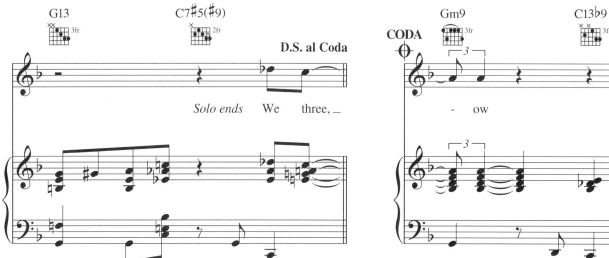

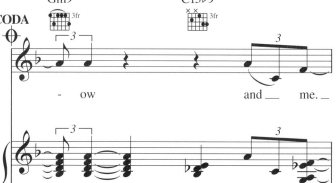

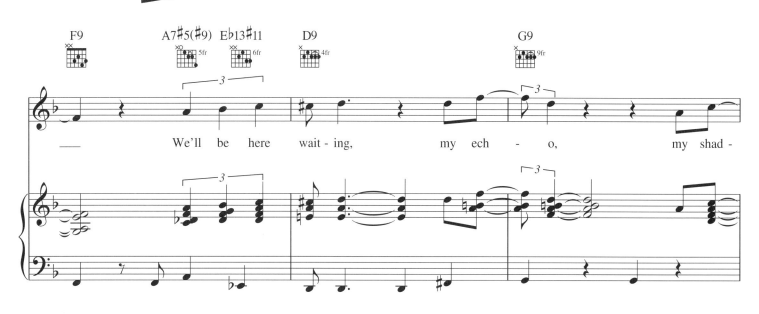

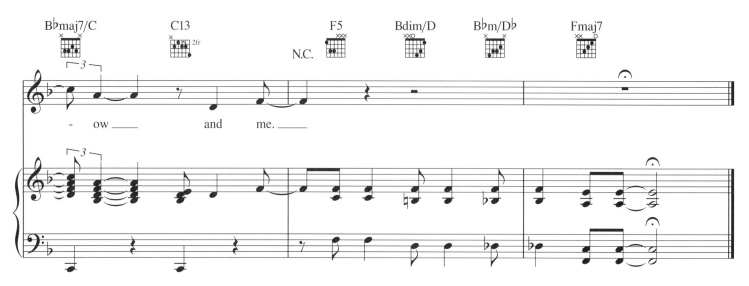

AC-CENT-TCHU-ATE THE POSITIVE

from the Motion Picture HERE COME THE WAVES

Lyric by JOHNNY MERCER
Music by HAROLD ARLEN

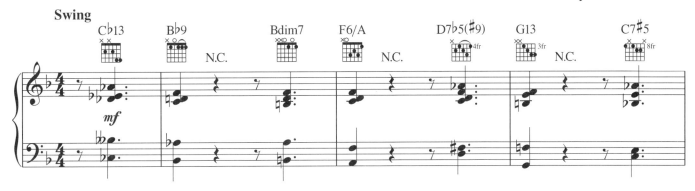

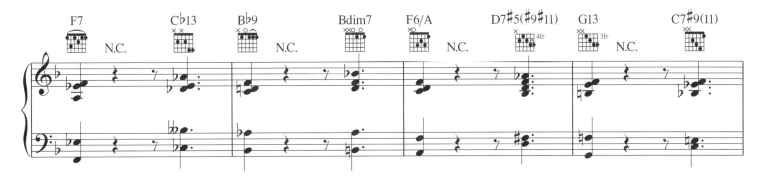

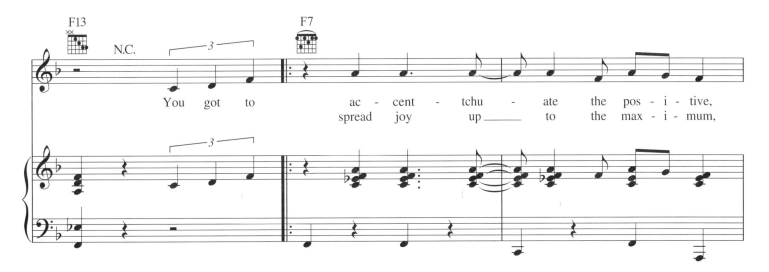

You got to ac - cent - tchu - ate the pos - i - tive,
spread joy up____ to the max - i - mum,

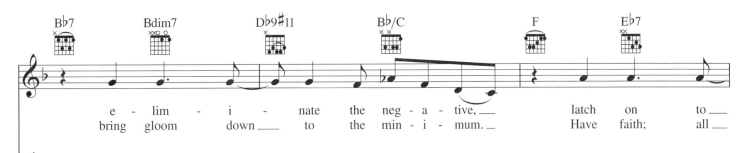

e - lim - i - nate the neg - a - tive,___ latch on to____
bring gloom down____ to the min - i - mum.___ Have faith; all____

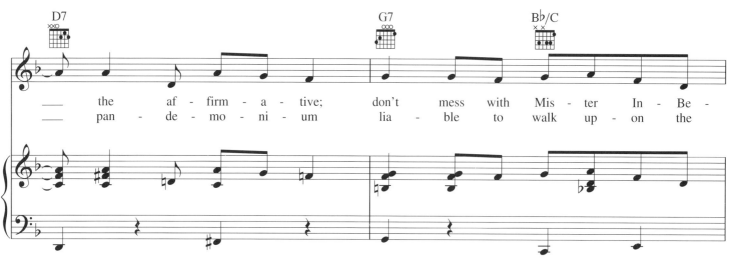

the af - firm - a - tive; don't mess with Mis - ter In - Be -
pan - de - mo - ni - um lia - ble to walk up - on the

tween. You got to scene. To il - lus - trate my last re -

mark: Jo - nah in the whale and No - ah in the ark, _____ what did they

do just when ev - 'ry - thing seemed so dark? ___

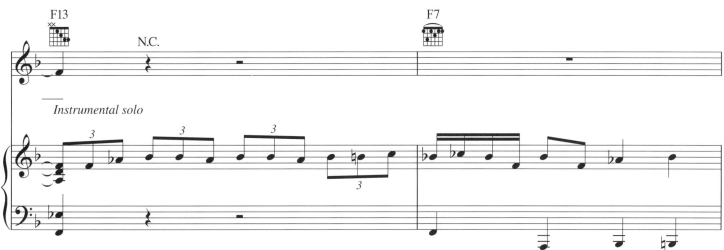

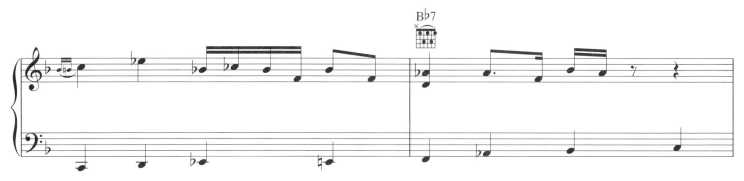

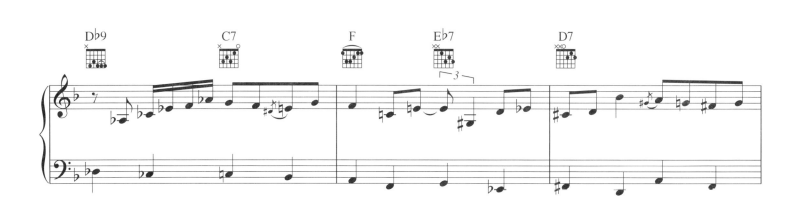

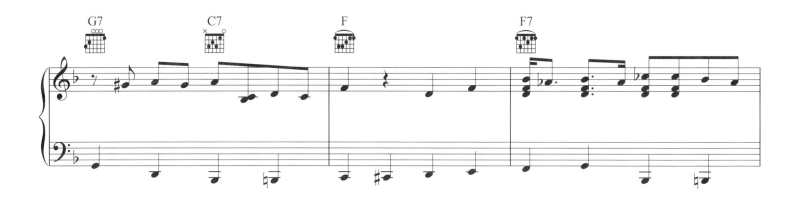

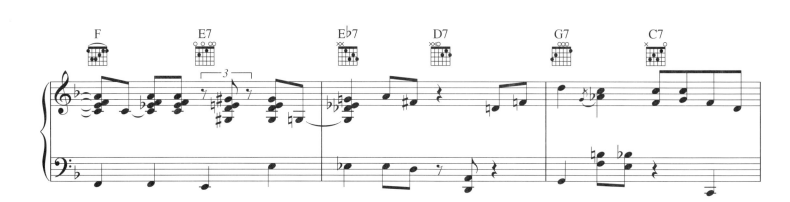

D.S. al Coda

Solo ends To il - lus - trate my last re - mark: ___ Jo - nah in the

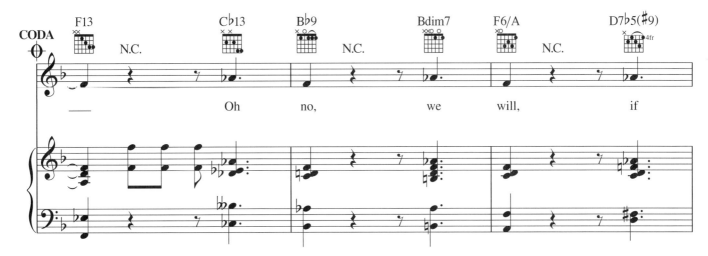

CODA

___ Oh no, we will, if

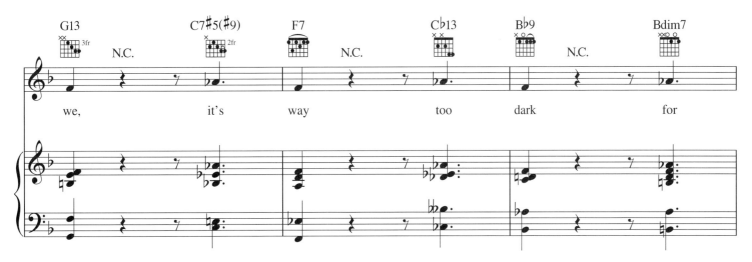

we, it's way too dark for

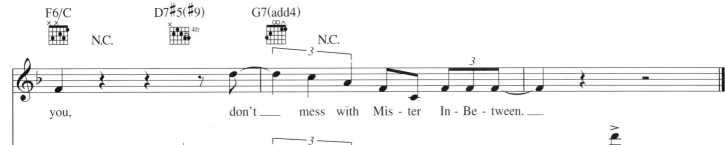

you, don't ___ mess with Mis - ter In - Be - tween. ___

MY VALENTINE

Words and Music by
PAUL McCARTNEY

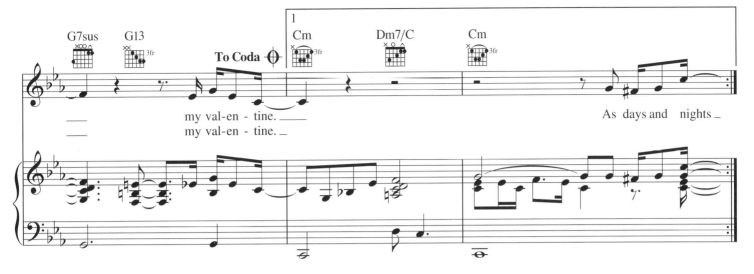

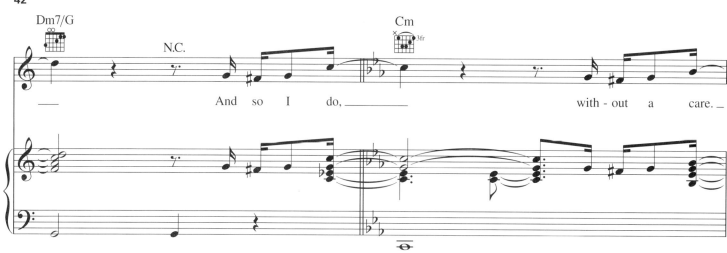

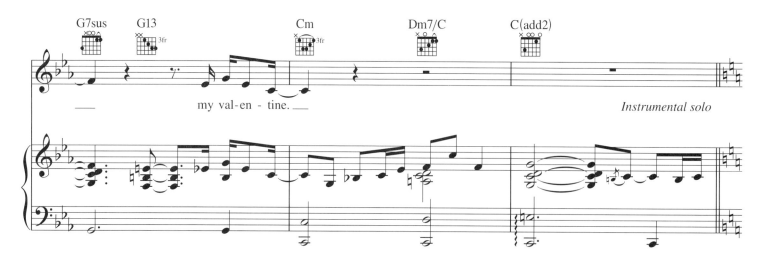

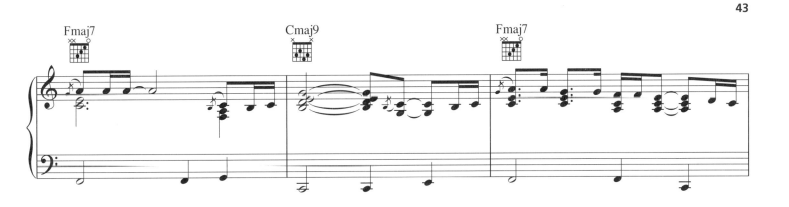

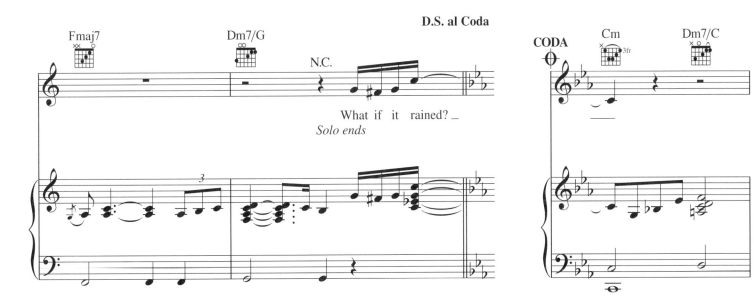

D.S. al Coda

N.C.

What if it rained? _

Solo ends

CODA

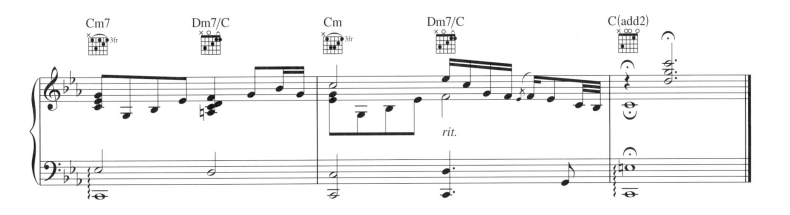

rit.

ALWAYS

Words and Music by
IRVING BERLIN

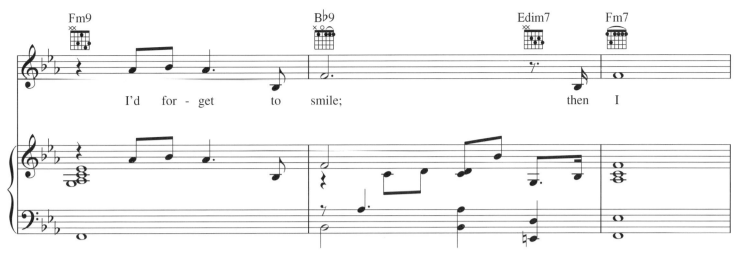

I'd for-get to smile; then I

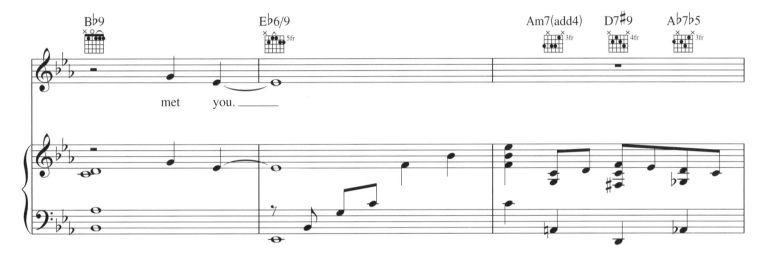

met you. _____

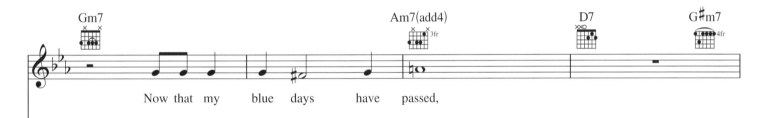

Now that my blue days have passed,

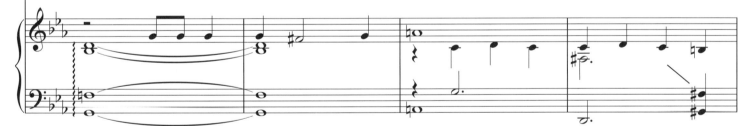

now that I've found you at last...

Slow Swing

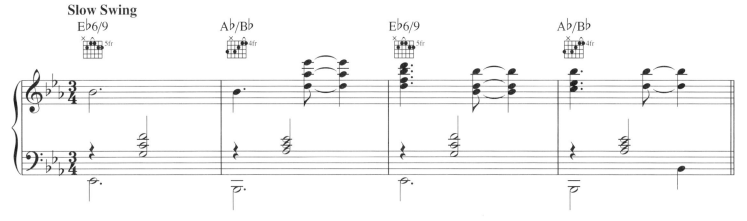

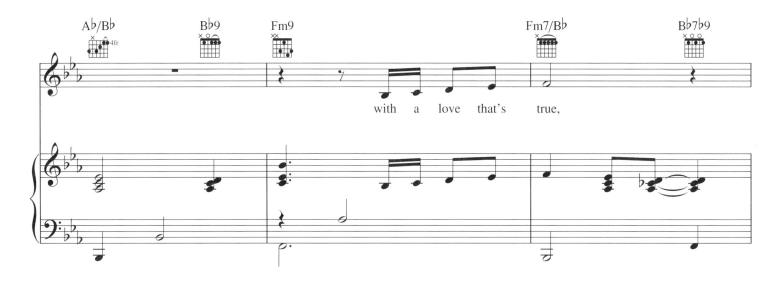

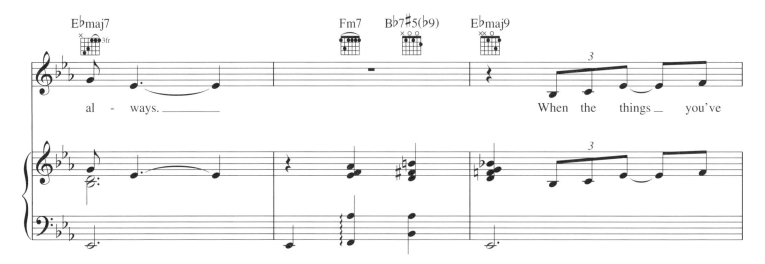

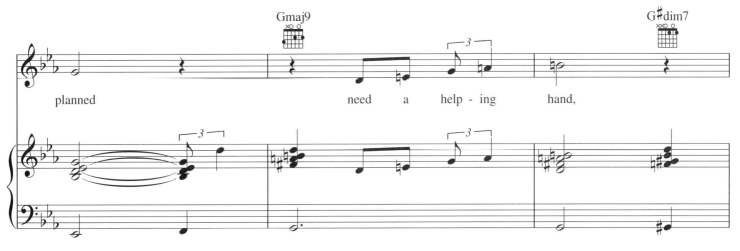

planned   need a help-ing hand,

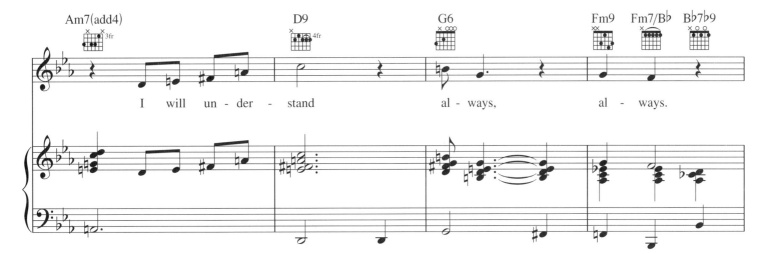

I will un-der-stand   al - ways,   al - ways.

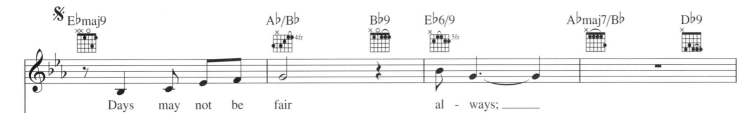

Days may not be fair   al - ways; _____

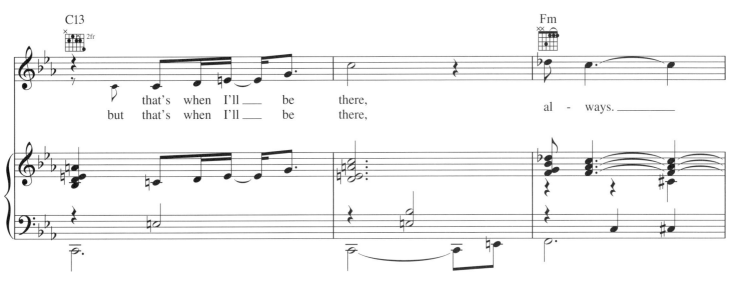

that's when I'll __ be there,
but that's when I'll __ be there,   al - ways. _____

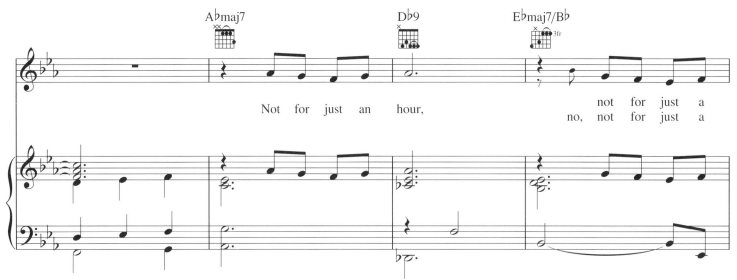

Not for just an hour,
not for just a

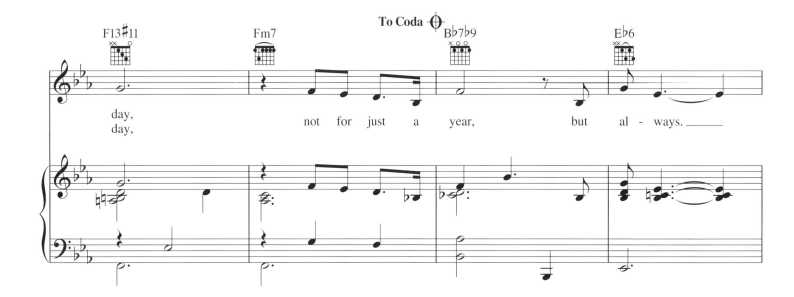

day,
day,

not for just a year, but al - ways. _____

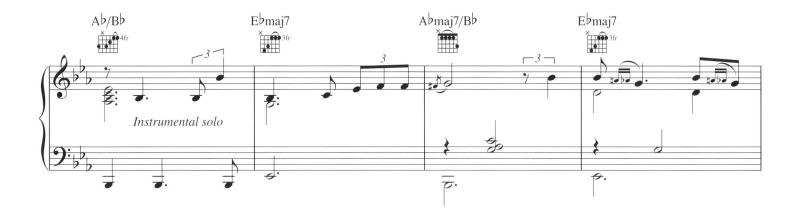

Instrumental solo

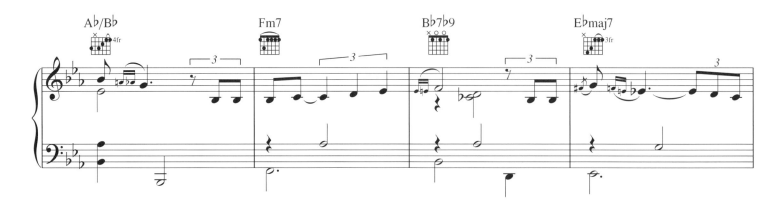

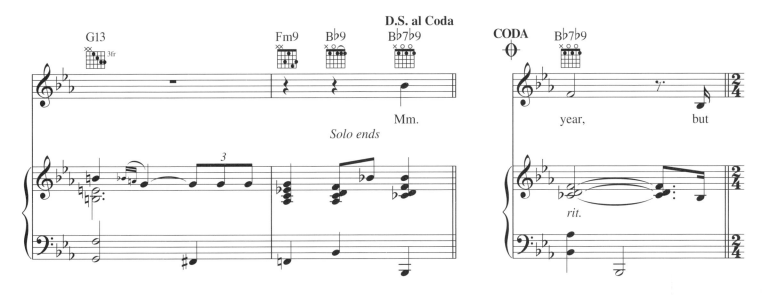

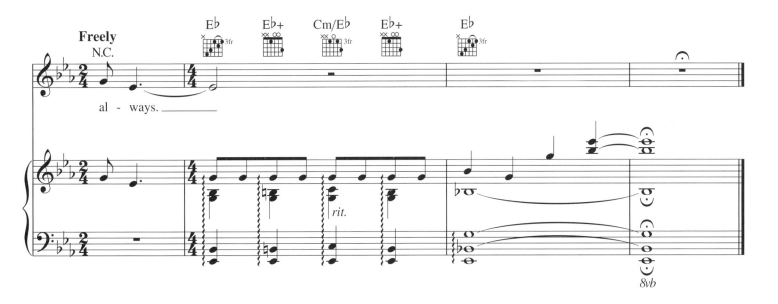

MY VERY GOOD FRIEND, THE MILKMAN

Words by JOHNNY BURKE
Music by HAROLD SPINA

Relaxed Swing

With pedal

Ah, my ver-y good friend the milk-man says ___ that
ver-y good friend the mail-man says ___ that

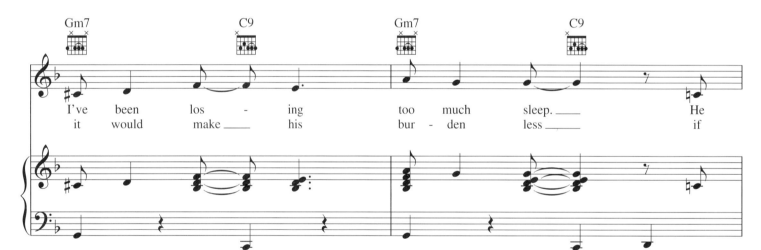

I've been los - ing too much sleep. ___ He
it would make ___ his bur - den less ___ if

does - n't like ___ the hours ___ I keep, ___ and he sug - gests ___ that
we both had ___ the same ad - dress, ___ and he sug - gests ___ that

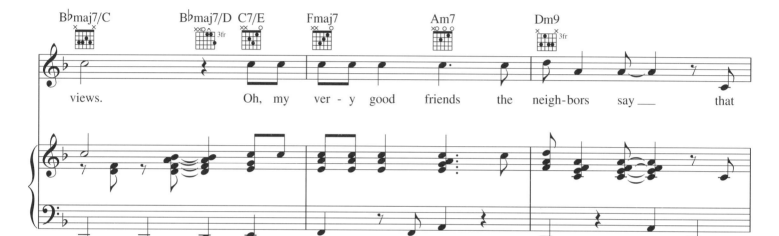

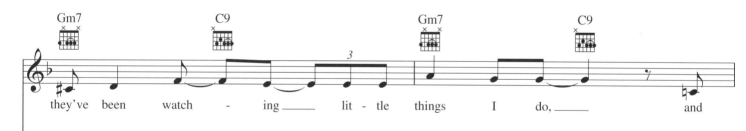

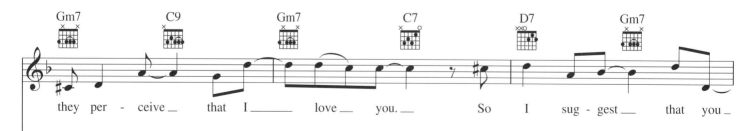

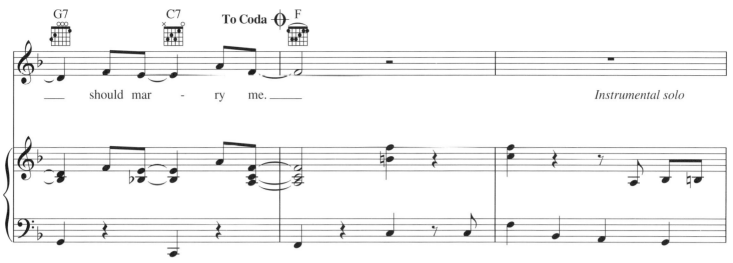

should mar - ry me. _____

Instrumental solo

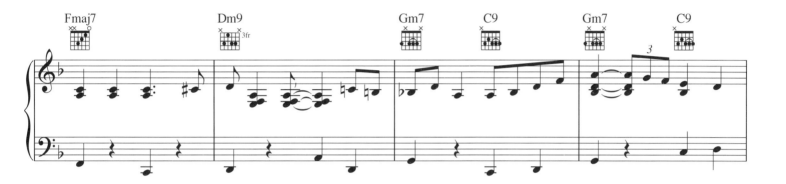

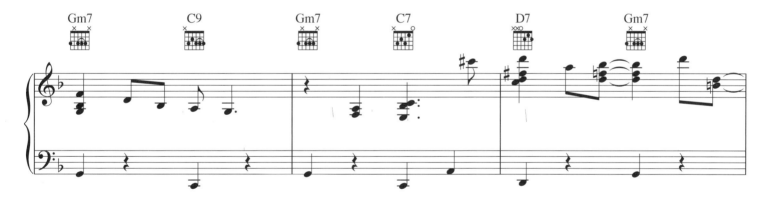

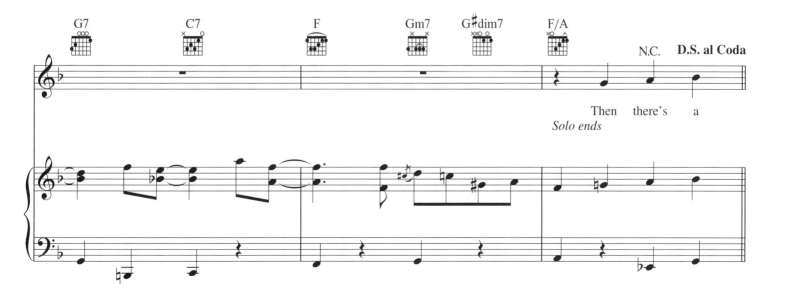

Then there's a

Solo ends

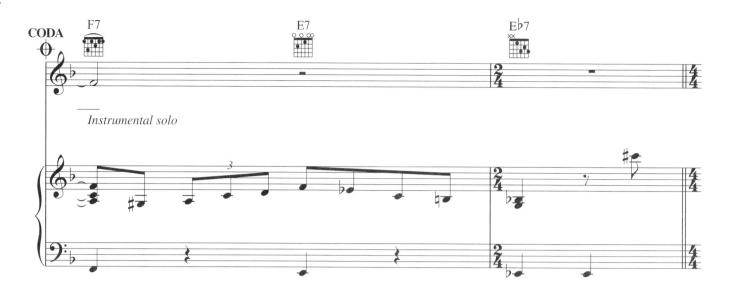

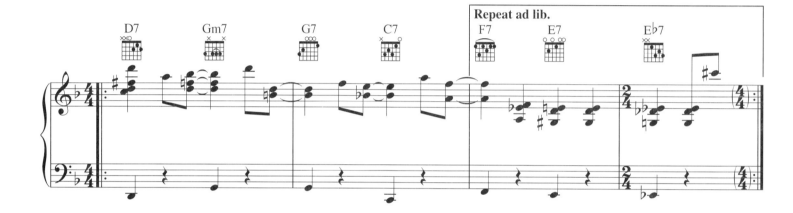

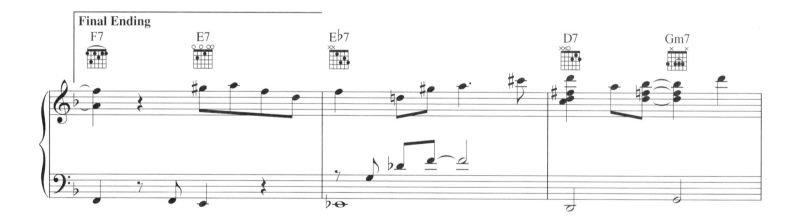

BYE BYE BLACKBIRD

from PETE KELLY'S BLUES

Lyric by MORT DIXON
Music by RAY HENDERSON

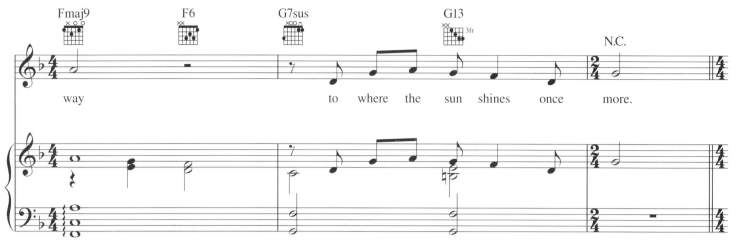

way to where the sun shines once more.

Slow Swing

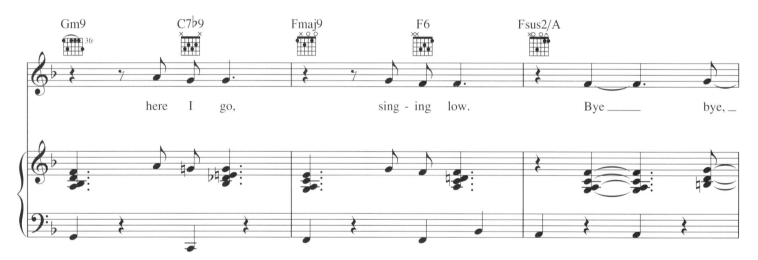

I'll pack up all my cares and woe; __

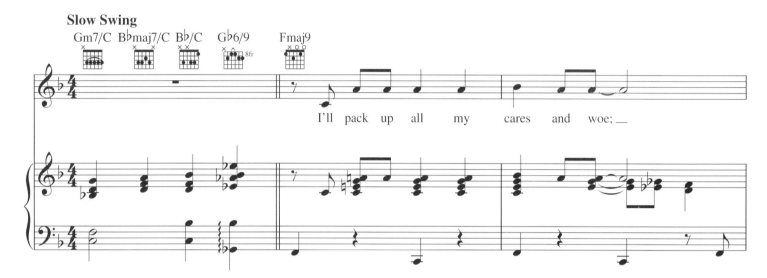

here I go, sing - ing low. Bye ____ bye, __

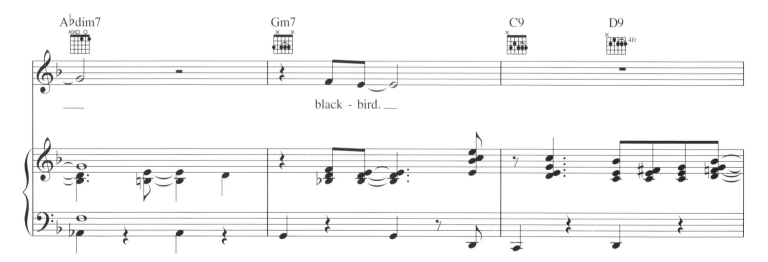

____ black - bird. __

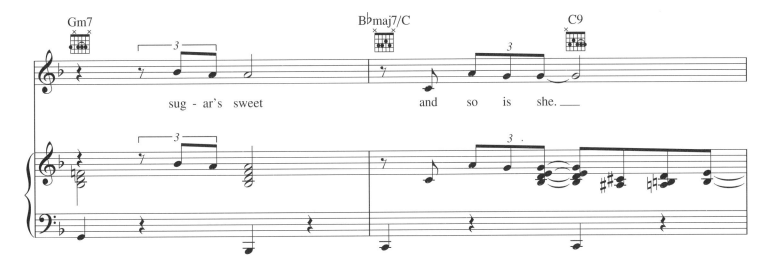

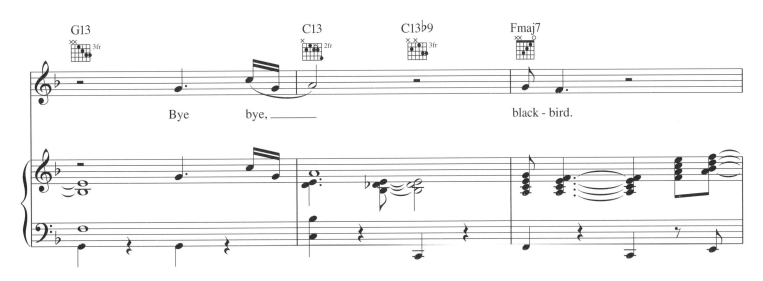

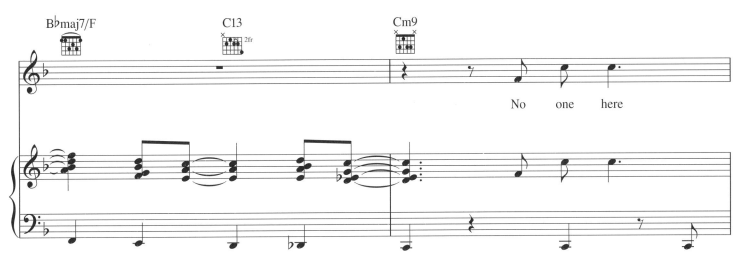

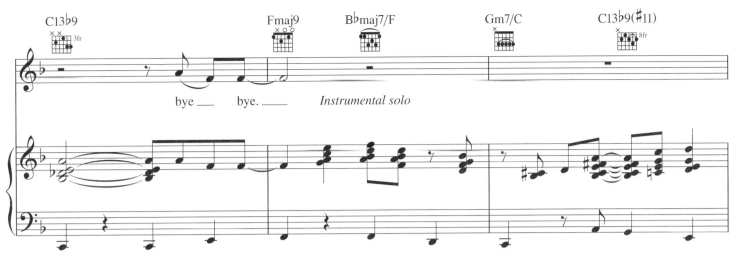

bye ___ bye. ___ *Instrumental solo*

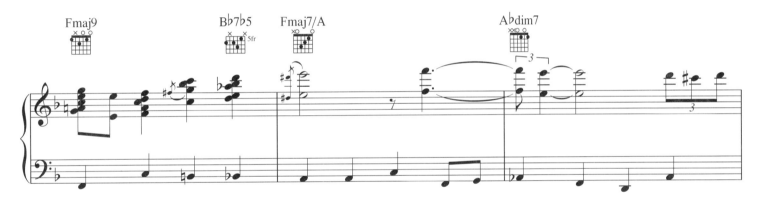

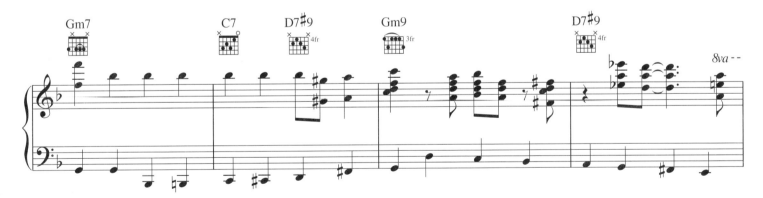

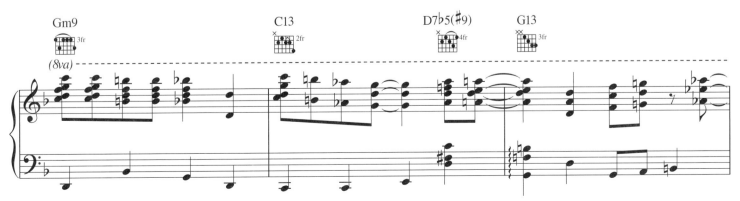

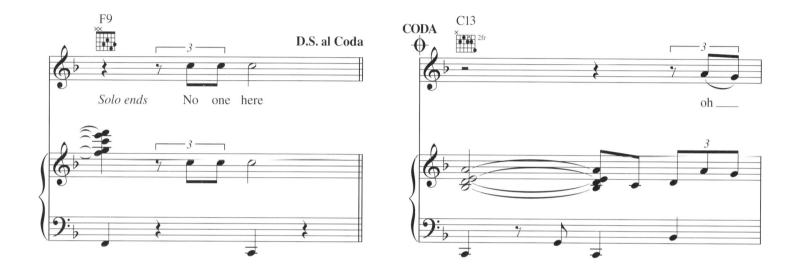

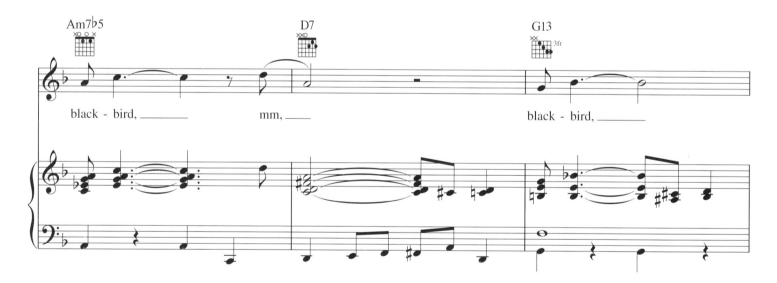

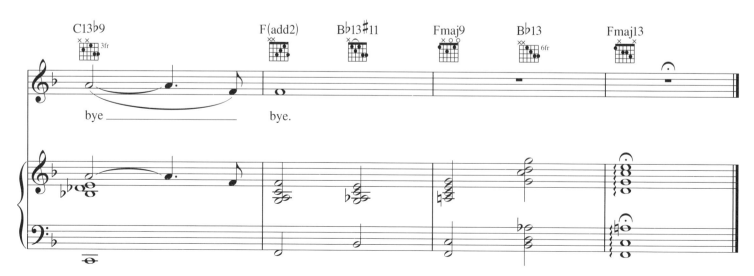

GET YOURSELF ANOTHER FOOL

Words and Music by FRANK HAYWOOD
and ERNEST TUCKER

Slow bluesy Swing

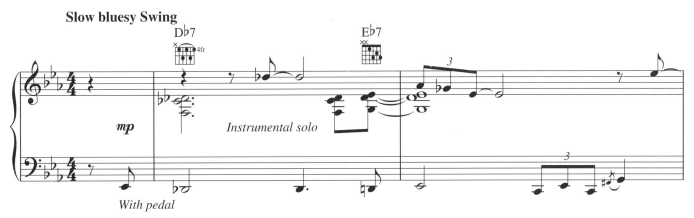

Instrumental solo

mp

With pedal

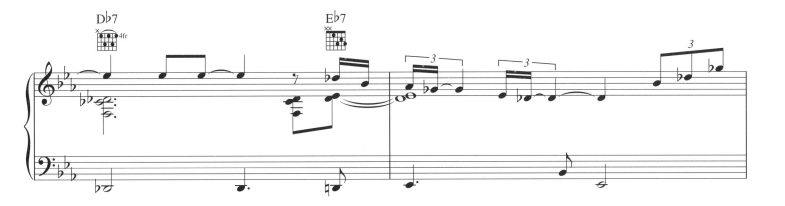

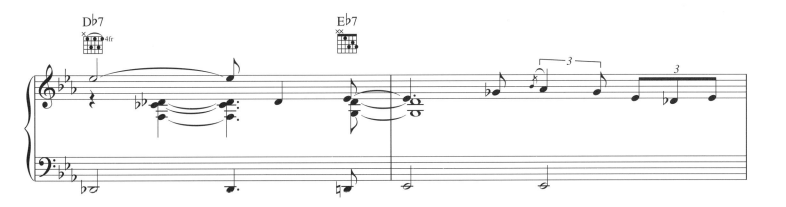

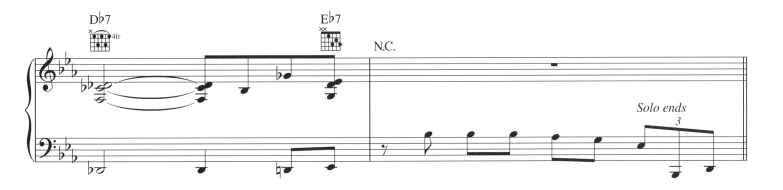

Solo ends

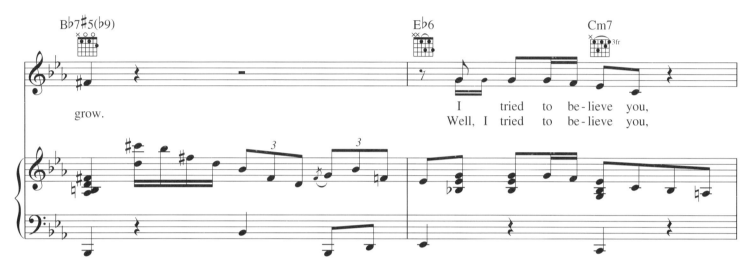

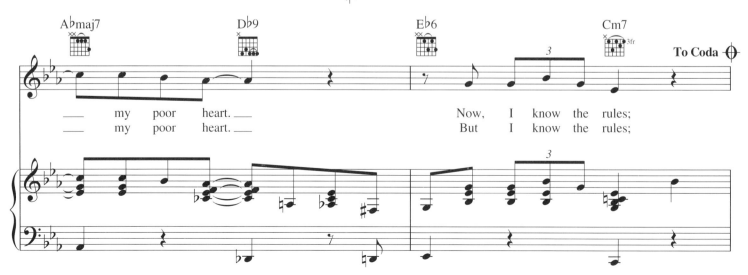

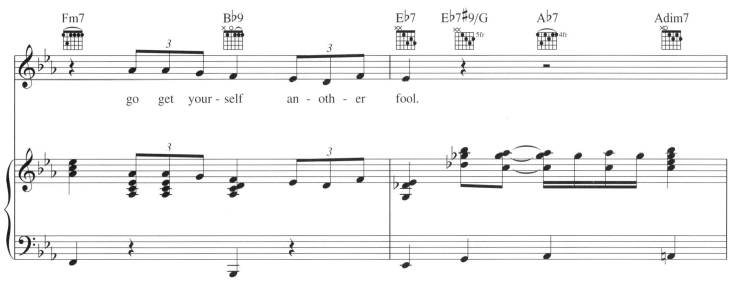

go get your-self an - oth - er fool.

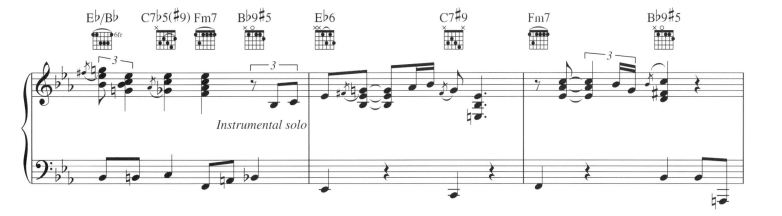

Instrumental solo

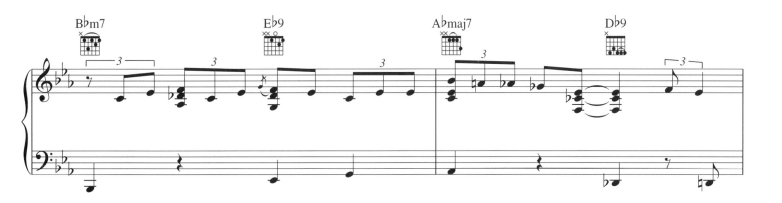

THE INCH WORM

from the Motion Picture HANS CHRISTIAN ANDERSEN

By FRANK LOESSER

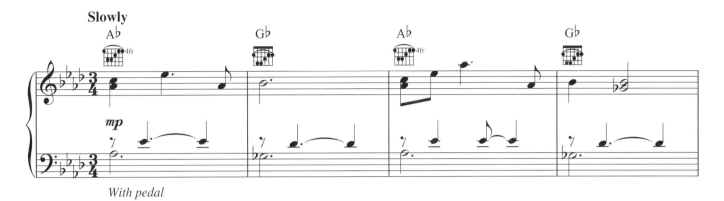

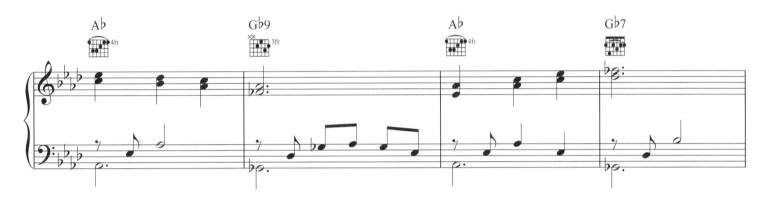

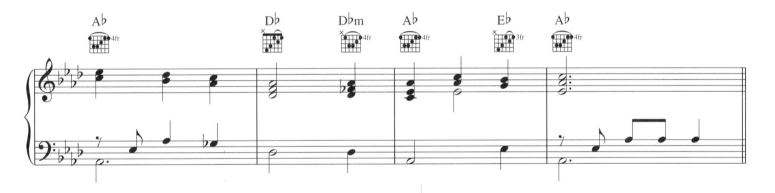

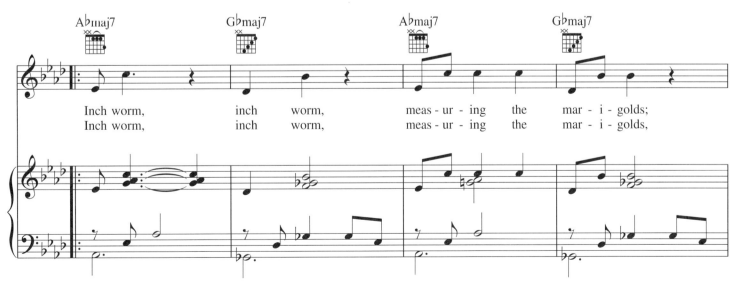

Inch worm, inch worm, meas-ur-ing the mar-i-golds;
Inch worm, inch worm, meas-ur-ing the mar-i-golds,

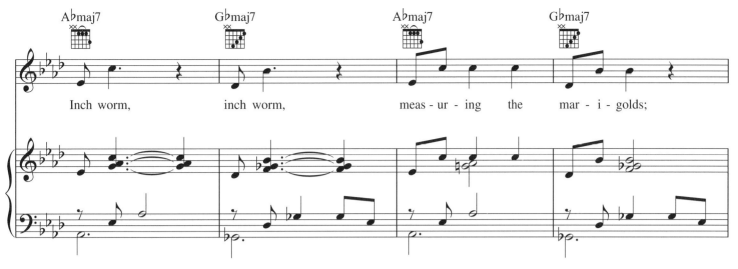

Inch worm, inch worm, meas - ur - ing the mar - i - golds;

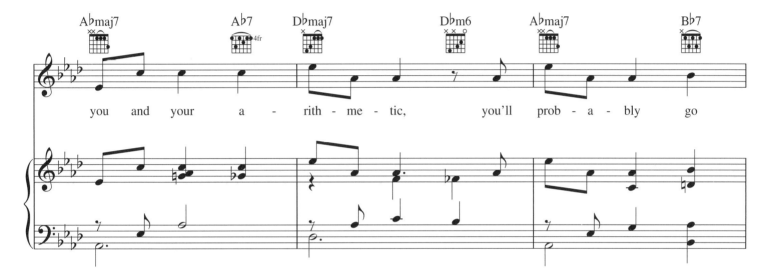

you and your a - rith - me - tic, you'll prob - a - bly go

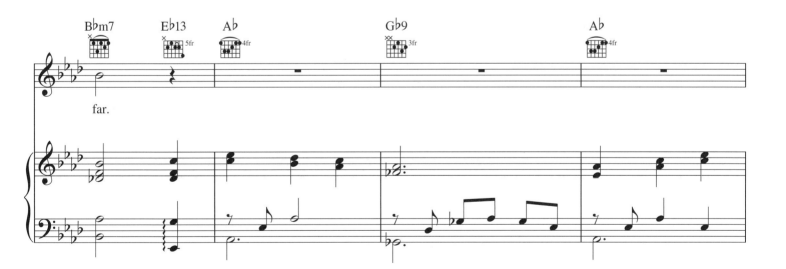

far.

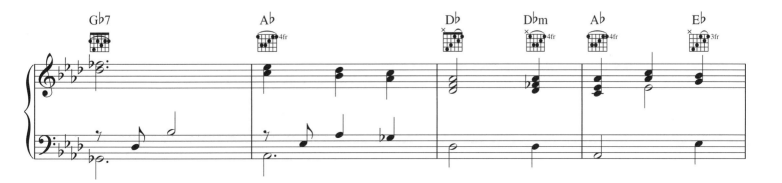

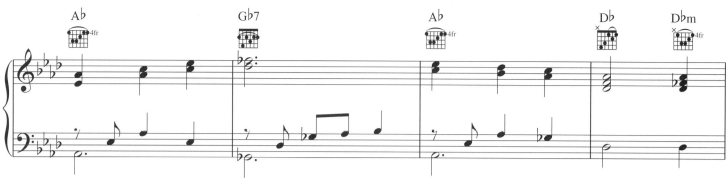

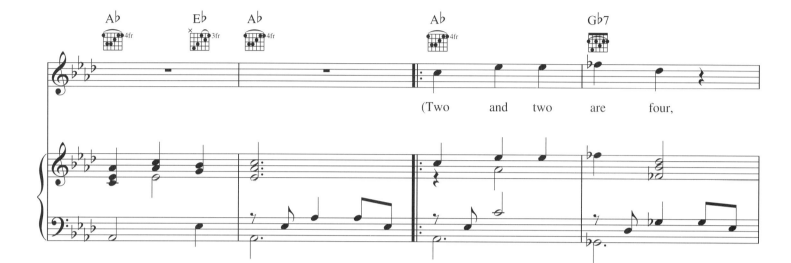

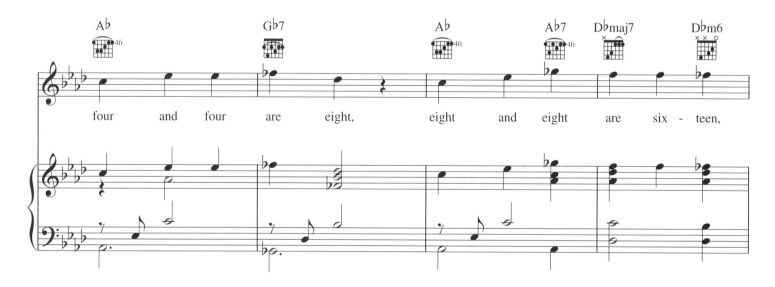

ONLY OUR HEARTS

Words and Music by
PAUL McCARTNEY

Slow Swing

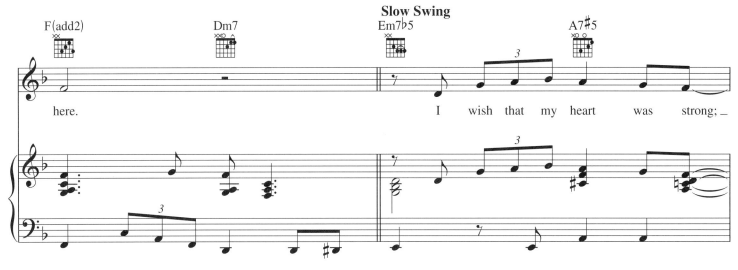

here.

I wish that my heart was strong; ___

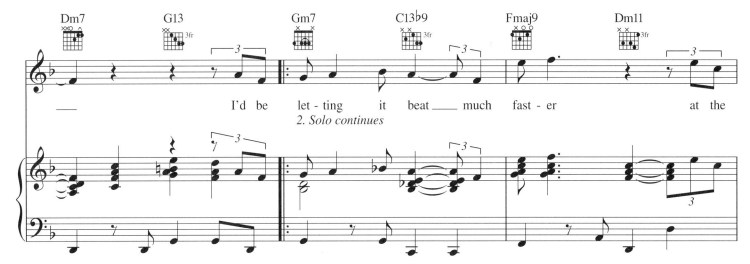

___ I'd be let - ting it beat ___ much fast - er   at the

2. Solo continues

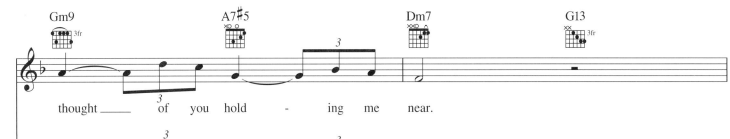

thought ___ of you hold - ing me near.

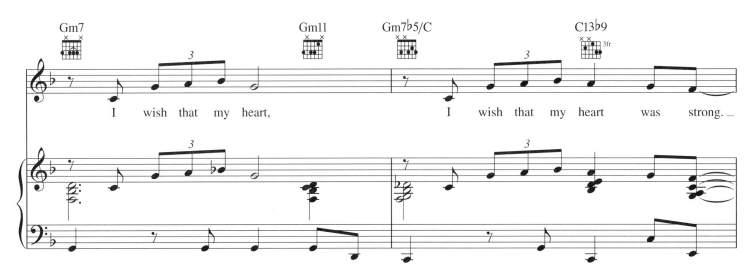

I wish that my heart,   I wish that my heart was strong. ___

Solo ends

Hop - ing to be ___ where you are;

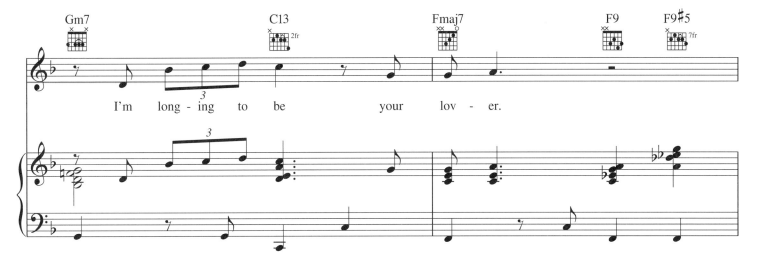

I'm long - ing to be your lov - er.

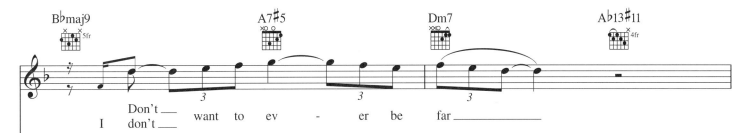

Don't ___ want to ev - er be far ___
I don't ___

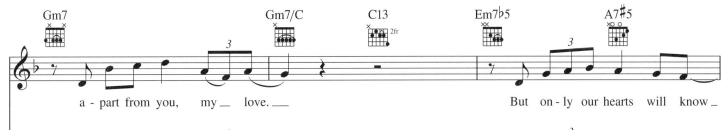

a - part from you, my ___ love. ___ But on - ly our hearts will know ___

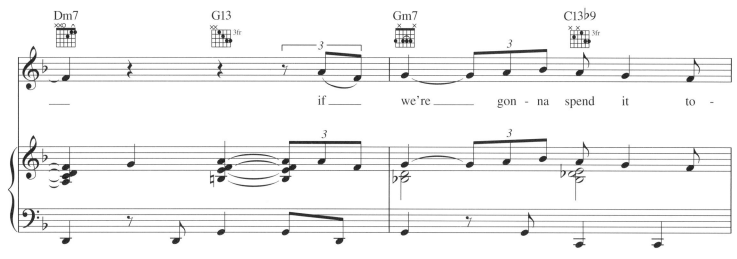

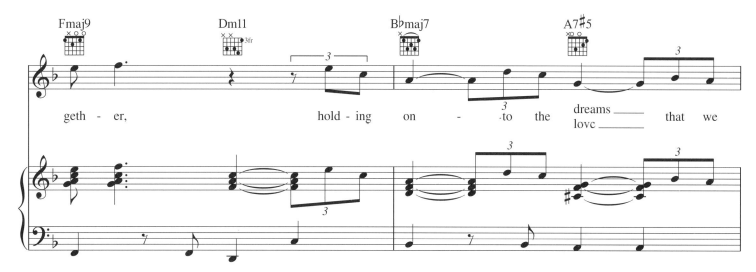